MznLnx

Missing Links Exam Preps

Exam Prep for

International Management: Managing Across Borders and Cultures

Deresky, 6th Edition

The MznLnx Exam Prep is your link from the texbook and lecture to your exams.
The MznLnx Exam Preps are unauthorized and comprehensive reviews of your textbooks.

All material provided by MznLnx and Rico Publications (c) 2010
Textbook publishers and textbook authors do not particpate in or contribute to these reviews.

MznLnx

Rico
Publications

Exam Prep for International Management: Managing Across Borders and Cultures
6th Edition
Deresky

Publisher: Raymond Houge
Assistant Editor: Michael Rouger
Text and Cover Designer: Lisa Buckner
Marketing Manager: Sara Swagger
Project Manager, Editorial Production: Jerry Emerson
Art Director: Vernon Lowerui

Product Manager: Dave Mason
Editorial Assitant: Rachel Guzmanji
Pedagogy: Debra Long
Cover Image: Jim Reed/Getty Images
Text and Cover Printer: City Printing, Inc.
Compositor: Media Mix, Inc.

(c) 2010 Rico Publications
ALL RIGHTS RESERVED. No part of this work
covered by the copyright may be reproduced or
used in any form or by an means--graphic, electronic,
or mechanical, including photocopying, recording,
taping, Web distribution, information storage, and
retrieval systems, or in any other manner--without the
written permission of the publisher.

For more information about our products, contact us at:
Dave.Mason@RicoPublications.com

For permission to use material from this text or
product, submit a request online to:
Dave.Mason@RicoPublications.com

Printed in the United States
ISBN:

Contents

CHAPTER 1
Assessing the Environment: Political, Economic, Legal, Technological — 1

CHAPTER 2
Managing Interdependence: Social Responsibility and Ethics — 6

CHAPTER 3
Understanding the Role of Culture — 10

CHAPTER 4
Communicating Across Cultures — 13

CHAPTER 5
Cross-cultural Negotiation and Decision Making — 15

CHAPTER 6
Formulating Strategy — 18

CHAPTER 7
Global Alliances and Strategy Implementation — 24

CHAPTER 8
Organization Structure and Control Systems — 28

CHAPTER 9
Staffing, Training, and Compensation for Global Operations — 31

CHAPTER 10
Developing a Global Management Cadre — 35

CHAPTER 11
Motivating and Leading — 39

ANSWER KEY — 43

TO THE STUDENT

COMPREHENSIVE

The *MznLnx* Exam Prep series is designed to help you pass your exams. Editors at MznLnx review your textbooks and then prepare these practice exams to help you master the textbook material. Unlike study guides, workbooks, and practice tests provided by the texbook publisher and textbook authors, *MznLnx* gives you **all** of the material in each chapter in exam form, not just samples, so you can be sure to nail your exam.

MECHANICAL

The MznLnx Exam Prep series creates exams that will help you learn the subject matter as well as test you on your understanding. Each question is designed to help you master the concept. Just working through the exams, you gain an understanding of the subject--its a simple mechanical process that produces success.

INTEGRATED STUDY GUIDE AND REVIEW

MznLnx is not just a set of exams designed to test you, its also a comprehensive review of the subject content. Each exam question is also a review of the concept, making sure that you will get the answer correct without having to go to other sources of material. You learn as you go! Its the easiest way to pass an exam.

HUMOR

Studying can be tedious and dry. MznLnx's instructional design includes moderate humor within the exam questions on occassion, to break the tedium and revitalize the brain

Chapter 1. Assessing the Environment: Political, Economic, Legal, Technological

1. _____ is the concept of how effective an organization is in achieving the outcomes the organization intends to produce. The idea of _____ is especially important for non-profit organizations as most people who donate money to non-profit organizations and charities are interested in knowing whether the organization is effective in accomplishing its goals.

An organization's effectiveness is also dependent on its communicative competence and ethics.

   a. Organizational structure
   b. Organizational development
   c. Organizational Effectiveness
   d. Informal organization

2. _____ was a writer, management consultant, and self-described 'social ecologist.' Widely considered to be 'the father of modern management,' his 39 books and countless scholarly and popular articles explored how humans are organized across all sectors of society--in business, government and the nonprofit world. His writings have predicted many of the major developments of the late twentieth century, including privatization and decentralization; the rise of Japan to economic world power; the decisive importance of marketing; and the emergence of the information society with its necessity of lifelong learning. In 1959, Drucker coined the term 'knowledge worker' and later in his life considered knowledge work productivity to be the next frontier of management.
   a. Debora L. Spar
   b. Chrissie Hynde
   c. Jacques Al-Salawat Nasruddin Nasser
   d. Peter Ferdinand Drucker

3. A _____ is an entity formed between two or more parties to undertake economic activity together. The parties agree to create a new entity by both contributing equity, and they then share in the revenues, expenses, and control of the enterprise. The venture can be for one specific project only, or a continuing business relationship such as the Fuji Xerox _____.
   a. Meritor Savings Bank v. Vinson
   b. Civil Rights Act of 1991
   c. Patent
   d. Joint Venture

4. An _____ is a person who has possession of an enterprise and assumes significant accountability for the inherent risks and the outcome. It is an ambitious leader who combines land, labor, and capital to create and market new goods or services. The term is a loanword from French and was first defined by the Irish economist Richard Cantillon.

a. A4e
b. A Stake in the Outcome
c. AAAI
d. Entrepreneur

5. _____ is a type of trade policy that allows traders to act and transact without interference from government. Thus, the policy permits trading partners mutual gains from trade, with goods and services produced according to the theory of comparative advantage.

Under a _____ policy, prices are a reflection of true supply and demand, and are the sole determinant of resource allocation.

a. 33 Strategies of War
b. 28-hour day
c. 1990 Clean Air Act
d. Free Trade

6. _____ is a designated group of countries that have agreed to eliminate tariffs, quotas and preferences on most (if not all) goods and services traded between them. It can be considered the second stage of economic integration. Countries choose this kind of economic integration form if their economical structures are complementary.

a. 33 Strategies of War
b. 1990 Clean Air Act
c. 28-hour day
d. Free trade area

7. The _____ is a trilateral trade bloc in North America created by the governments of the United States, Canada, and Mexico. The agreement creating the trade bloc came into force on January 1, 1994. It superseded the Canada-United States Free Trade Agreement between the U.S. and Canada.

a. Business war game
b. Trade union
c. North American Free Trade Agreement
d. Career portfolios

8. A _____ is a country that has low standards of democratic governments, civil service, industrialization, social programs, and/or human rights guarantees that are yet to 'develop' to those met in the West or alternative goals of material progress (not necessarily a clone of those of the West.) It is often a term used to describe a nation with a low level of material well being. Despite this definition, the levels of development may vary, with some developing countries having higher average standards of living.

a. 33 Strategies of War
b. Developing country
c. 28-hour day
d. 1990 Clean Air Act

9. _____ refers to the stock of skills and knowledge embodied in the ability to perform labor so as to produce economic value. It is the skills and knowledge gained by a worker through education and experience. Many early economic theories refer to it simply as labor, one of three factors of production, and consider it to be a fungible resource -- homogeneous and easily interchangeable.

a. Deflation
b. Market structure
c. Productivity management
d. Human capital

10. A _____ or transnational corporation is a corporation or enterprise that manages production or delivers services in more than one country. It can also be referred to as an international corporation.

The first modern _____ is generally thought to be the Dutch East India Company, established in 1602.

a. Multinational corporation
b. Command center
c. Small and medium enterprises
d. Financial Accounting Standards Board

11. _____ in its literal sense is the process of transformation of local or regional phenomena into global ones. It can be described as a process by which the people of the world are unified into a single society and function together.

This process is a combination of economic, technological, sociocultural and political forces.

a. Cost Management
b. Collaborative Planning, Forecasting and Replenishment
c. Globalization
d. Histogram

12. In decision theory and estimation theory, the _____ of an estimator, $\hat{\theta}$, of an unknown parameter of the distribution, θ, is the expected value of the loss function

$$R(\theta, \hat{\theta}) = \mathbb{E}_\theta L(\theta, \hat{\theta}) = \int L(\theta, \hat{\theta})\, dP_\theta.$$

where dP_θ is a probability measure parametrized by θ.

- For a scalar parameter θ and a quadratic loss function,

$$L(\theta, \hat{\theta}) = (\theta - \hat{\theta})^2$$

the _____ function becomes the mean squared error of the estimate,

$$R(\theta, \hat{\theta}) = E_\theta(\theta - \hat{\theta})^2$$

- In density estimation, the unknown parameter is probability density itself. The loss function is typically chosen to be a norm in an appropriate function space. For example, for L^2 norm,

$$L(f, \hat{f}) = \|f - \hat{f}\|_2^2$$

the _____ function becomes the mean integrated squared error

$$R(f, \hat{f}) = E\|f - \hat{f}\|^2$$

a. Risk
b. Linear model
c. Risk aversion
d. Financial modeling

13. _____, commonly referred to as 'eBusiness' or 'e-Business', may be defined as the utilization of information and communication technologies (ICT) in support of all the activities of business. Commerce constitutes the exchange of products and services between businesses, groups and individuals and hence can be seen as one of the essential activities of any business. Hence, electronic commerce or eCommerce focuses on the use of ICT to enable the external activities and relationships of the business with individuals, groups and other businesses .
   a. Electronic business
   b. A Stake in the Outcome
   c. AAAI
   d. A4e

Chapter 1. Assessing the Environment: Political, Economic, Legal, Technological   5

14. _____ describes commerce transactions between businesses, such as between a manufacturer and a wholesaler, or between a wholesaler and a retailer. Contrasting terms are business-to-consumer (B2C) and business-to-government (B2G.)

The volume of B2B transactions is much higher than the volume of B2C transactions.

   a. Market environment
   b. Product bundling
   c. Category management
   d. Business-to-business

15. Business-to-consumer describes activities of businesses serving end consumers with products and/or services.

An example of a _____ transaction would be a person buying a pair of shoes from a retailer. The transactions that led to the shoes being available for purchase, that is the purchase of the leather, laces, rubber, etc.

   a. PEST analysis
   b. Market environment
   c. Green marketing
   d. B2C

16. _____, commonly known as e-commerce, consists of the buying and selling of products or services over electronic systems such as the Internet and other computer networks. The amount of trade conducted electronically has grown extraordinarily with widespread Internet usage. The use of commerce is conducted in this way, spurring and drawing on innovations in electronic funds transfer, supply chain management, Internet marketing, online transaction processing, electronic data interchange (EDI), inventory management systems, and automated data collection systems.

   a. A4e
   b. A Stake in the Outcome
   c. Online shopping
   d. Electronic Commerce

Chapter 2. Managing Interdependence: Social Responsibility and Ethics

1. _____ is a form of corporate self-regulation integrated into a business model. Ideally, _____ policy would function as a built-in, self-regulating mechanism whereby business would monitor and ensure their adherence to law, ethical standards, and international norms. Business would embrace responsibility for the impact of their activities on the environment, consumers, employees, communities, stakeholders and all other members of the public sphere.
   a. 28-hour day
   b. 33 Strategies of War
   c. 1990 Clean Air Act
   d. Corporate social responsibility

2. A _____ or transnational corporation is a corporation or enterprise that manages production or delivers services in more than one country. It can also be referred to as an international corporation.

The first modern _____ is generally thought to be the Dutch East India Company, established in 1602.

   a. Financial Accounting Standards Board
   b. Small and medium enterprises
   c. Command center
   d. Multinational corporation

3. Organizational culture is not the same as _____. It is wider and deeper concepts, something that an organization 'is' rather than what it 'has' (according to Buchanan and Huczynski.)

_____ is the total sum of the values, customs, traditions and meanings that make a company unique.

   a. Path-goal theory
   b. Job analysis
   c. Work design
   d. Corporate culture

4. In philosophy _____ is the position that moral or ethical propositions do not reflect objective and/or universal moral truths, but instead make claims relative to social, cultural, historical or personal circumstances. Moral relativists hold that no universal standard exists by which to assess an ethical proposition's truth. Relativistic positions often see moral values as applicable only within certain cultural boundaries (cultural relativism) or in the context of individual preferences (individualist ethical subjectivism.)
   a. Moral absolutism
   b. 1990 Clean Air Act
   c. Moral relativism
   d. 28-hour day

Chapter 2. Managing Interdependence: Social Responsibility and Ethics

5. _____ is a form of applied ethics that examines ethical principles and moral or ethical problems that arise in a business environment. It applies to all aspects of business conduct and is relevant to the conduct of individuals and business organizations as a whole. Applied ethics is a field of ethics that deals with ethical questions in many fields such as medical, technical, legal and _____.
   a. Hypernorms
   b. Facilitation payments
   c. Corporate Sustainability
   d. Business Ethics

6. _____ is a dynamic of being mutually and physically responsible to and sharing a common set of principles with others. This concept differs distinctly from 'dependence' in that an interdependent relationship implies that all participants are emotionally, economically, ecologically and or morally 'interdependent.' Some people advocate freedom or independence as a sort of ultimate good; others do the same with devotion to one's family, community, or society. _____ recognizes the truth in each position and weaves them together.
   a. A Stake in the Outcome
   b. Interdependence
   c. AAAI
   d. A4e

7. The _____ of 1977 (15 U.S.C. §§ 78dd-1, et seq.) is a United States federal law known primarily for two of its main provisions, one that addresses accounting transparency requirements under the Securities Exchange Act of 1934 and another concerning bribery of foreign officials.
   a. Foreign Corrupt Practices Act
   b. Meritor Savings Bank v. Vinson
   c. Limited liability
   d. Social Security Act of 1965

8. _____ in its classic form is defined as a company from one country making a physical investment into building a factory in another country. It is the establishment of an enterprise by a foreigner. Its definition can be extended to include investments made to acquire lasting interest in enterprises operating outside of the economy of the investor.
   a. Compensation methods
   b. Business Roundtable
   c. Headquarters
   d. Foreign direct investment

9. _____ is a field of study that looks at how people from differing cultural backgrounds endeavour to communicate.

8 *Chapter 2. Managing Interdependence: Social Responsibility and Ethics*

In years during and preceding the Cold War, the United States economy was largely self-contained because the world was polarized into two separate and competing powers: the east and west. However, changes and advancements in economic relationships, political systems, and technological options began to break down old cultural barriers.

   a. 28-hour day
   b. Cross-cultural communication
   c. 33 Strategies of War
   d. 1990 Clean Air Act

10. The _____ is a trilateral trade bloc in North America created by the governments of the United States, Canada, and Mexico. The agreement creating the trade bloc came into force on January 1, 1994. It superseded the Canada-United States Free Trade Agreement between the U.S. and Canada.
   a. Business war game
   b. Career portfolios
   c. Trade union
   d. North American Free Trade Agreement

11. The field of _____ looks at the relationship between management and workers, particularly groups of workers represented by a union.

_____ is an important factor in analyzing 'varieties of capitalism', such as neocorporatism, social democracy, and neoliberalism

   a. Organizational effectiveness
   b. Overtime
   c. Informal organization
   d. Industrial relations

12. A _____ is an entity formed between two or more parties to undertake economic activity together. The parties agree to create a new entity by both contributing equity, and they then share in the revenues, expenses, and control of the enterprise. The venture can be for one specific project only, or a continuing business relationship such as the Fuji Xerox _____.
   a. Civil Rights Act of 1991
   b. Patent
   c. Meritor Savings Bank v. Vinson
   d. Joint Venture

Chapter 2. Managing Interdependence: Social Responsibility and Ethics

13. An _____ is a person who has possession of an enterprise and assumes significant accountability for the inherent risks and the outcome. It is an ambitious leader who combines land, labor, and capital to create and market new goods or services. The term is a loanword from French and was first defined by the Irish economist Richard Cantillon.
    a. Entrepreneur
    b. A Stake in the Outcome
    c. AAAI
    d. A4e

14. _____ is the concept of how effective an organization is in achieving the outcomes the organization intends to produce. The idea of _____ is especially important for non-profit organizations as most people who donate money to non-profit organizations and charities are interested in knowing whether the organization is effective in accomplishing its goals.

An organization's effectiveness is also dependent on its communicative competence and ethics.

   a. Organizational development
   b. Organizational Effectiveness
   c. Informal organization
   d. Organizational structure

Chapter 3. Understanding the Role of Culture

1. _____ is an idea in the field of Organizational studies and management which describes the psychology, attitudes, experiences, beliefs and Values (personal and cultural values) of an organization. It has been defined as 'the specific collection of values and norms that are shared by people and groups in an organization and that control the way they interact with each other and with stakeholders outside the organization.'

This definition continues to explain organizational values also known as 'beliefs and ideas about what kinds of goals members of an organization should pursue and ideas about the appropriate kinds or standards of behavior organizational members should use to achieve these goals. From organizational values develop organizational norms, guidelines or expectations that prescribe appropriate kinds of behavior by employees in particular situations and control the behavior of organizational members towards one another.'

_____ is not the same as corporate culture.

a. Union shop
b. Organizational development
c. Organizational effectiveness
d. Organizational culture

2. In sociology, anthropology and cultural studies, a _____ is a group of people with a culture (whether distinct or hidden) which differentiates them from the larger culture to which they belong. If a particular _____ is characterized by a systematic opposition to the dominant culture, it may be described as a counterculture.

As early as 1950, David Riesman distinguished between a majority, 'which passively accepted commercially provided styles and meanings, and a '_____' which actively sought a minority style ...

a. 1990 Clean Air Act
b. 28-hour day
c. 33 Strategies of War
d. Subculture

3. A _____ is an entity formed between two or more parties to undertake economic activity together. The parties agree to create a new entity by both contributing equity, and they then share in the revenues, expenses, and control of the enterprise. The venture can be for one specific project only, or a continuing business relationship such as the Fuji Xerox _____.
a. Patent
b. Meritor Savings Bank v. Vinson
c. Civil Rights Act of 1991
d. Joint Venture

Chapter 3. Understanding the Role of Culture

4. An _____ is a person who has possession of an enterprise and assumes significant accountability for the inherent risks and the outcome. It is an ambitious leader who combines land, labor, and capital to create and market new goods or services. The term is a loanword from French and was first defined by the Irish economist Richard Cantillon.
   a. Entrepreneur
   b. A Stake in the Outcome
   c. AAAI
   d. A4e

5. _____ is a trait taught by many personal development experts and psychotherapists and the subject of many popular self-help books. It is linked to self-esteem and considered an important communication skill.

As a communication style and strategy, _____ is distinguished from aggression and passivity.

   a. A4e
   b. Intrinsic motivation
   c. Assertiveness
   d. A Stake in the Outcome

6. _____ refers to the movement of cash into or out of a business or financial product. It is usually measured during a specified, finite period of time. Measurement of _____ can be used

   - to determine a project's rate of return or value. The time of _____s into and out of projects are used as inputs in financial models such as internal rate of return, and net present value.
   - to determine problems with a business's liquidity. Being profitable does not necessarily mean being liquid. A company can fail because of a shortage of cash, even while profitable.
   - as an alternate measure of a business's profits when it is believed that accrual accounting concepts do not represent economic realities. For example, a company may be notionally profitable but generating little operational cash (as may be the case for a company that barters its products rather than selling for cash.) In such a case, the company may be deriving additional operating cash by issuing shares evaluating default risk, re-investment requirements, etc.

_____ is a generic term used differently depending on the context. It may be defined by users for their own purposes.

   a. Gross profit margin
   b. Cash flow
   c. Sweat equity
   d. Gross profit

Chapter 3. Understanding the Role of Culture

7. _____ is a term used to describe any moral, political that stresses human interdependence and the importance of a collective, rather than the importance of separate individuals. Collectivists focus on community and society, and seek to give priority to group goals over individual goals. The philosophical underpinnings of _____ are for some related to holism or organicism - the view that the whole is greater than the sum of its parts/pieces.
   a. 28-hour day
   b. Collaborative methods
   c. 1990 Clean Air Act
   d. Collectivism

8. _____ is a practice whereby the employees have a role in management of a company. The word is a somewhat clumsy and literal translation from the German word Mitbestimmung. _____ rights are different in different legal environments.
   a. Business Process Improvement
   b. Management team
   c. Decentralization
   d. Co-determination

9. Various _____ can be employed dependent on the culture of the business, the nature of the task, the nature of the workforce and the personality and skills of the leaders. This idea was further developed by Robert Tannenbaum and Warren H. Schmidt (1958, 1973) who argued that the style of leadership is dependent upon the prevailing circumstance; therefore leaders should exercise a range of leadership styles and should deploy them as appropriate.

An Autocratic or authoritarian manager makes all the decisions, keeping the information and decision making among the senior management.

   a. 33 Strategies of War
   b. 1990 Clean Air Act
   c. Management styles
   d. 28-hour day

Chapter 4. Communicating Across Cultures

1. _____ refers to the movement of cash into or out of a business or financial product. It is usually measured during a specified, finite period of time. Measurement of _____ can be used

    - to determine a project's rate of return or value. The time of _____s into and out of projects are used as inputs in financial models such as internal rate of return, and net present value.
    - to determine problems with a business's liquidity. Being profitable does not necessarily mean being liquid. A company can fail because of a shortage of cash, even while profitable.
    - as an alternate measure of a business's profits when it is believed that accrual accounting concepts do not represent economic realities. For example, a company may be notionally profitable but generating little operational cash (as may be the case for a company that barters its products rather than selling for cash.) In such a case, the company may be deriving additional operating cash by issuing shares evaluating default risk, re-investment requirements, etc.

    _____ is a generic term used differently depending on the context. It may be defined by users for their own purposes.

    a. Gross profit margin
    b. Cash flow
    c. Gross profit
    d. Sweat equity

2. The term _____ was introduced by anthropologist Edward T. Hall in 1966 to describe set measurable distances between people as they interact. The effects of _____, according to Hall, can be summarized by the following loose rule:

    According to Jonathon Tabor distance-spacing theories based on the early animal-like human of German zoologist Heini Hediger, as found in his 1955 book Studies of the Behavior of Captive Animals in Zoos and Circuses. Hediger, in animals, had distinguished between flight distance , critical distance (attack boundary), personal distance (distance separating members of non-contact species, as a pair of swans), and social distance (intraspecies communication distance.)

    a. 33 Strategies of War
    b. 28-hour day
    c. Proxemics
    d. 1990 Clean Air Act

3. _____ is a field of study that looks at how people from differing cultural backgrounds endeavour to communicate.

    In years during and preceding the Cold War, the United States economy was largely self-contained because the world was polarized into two separate and competing powers: the east and west. However, changes and advancements in economic relationships, political systems, and technological options began to break down old cultural barriers.

a. 33 Strategies of War
b. 1990 Clean Air Act
c. Cross-cultural communication
d. 28-hour day

4. A _____, in business matters, is an entity that is controlled by a bigger and more powerful entity. The controlled entity is called a company, corporation, or limited liability company and in some cases can be a government or state-owned enterprise, and the controlling entity is called its parent (or the parent company.) The reason for this distinction is that a lone company cannot be a _____ of any organization; only an entity representing a legal fiction as a separate entity can be a _____.

a. Subsidiary
b. 33 Strategies of War
c. 1990 Clean Air Act
d. 28-hour day

Chapter 5. Cross-cultural Negotiation and Decision Making

1. A _____ is an entity formed between two or more parties to undertake economic activity together. The parties agree to create a new entity by both contributing equity, and they then share in the revenues, expenses, and control of the enterprise. The venture can be for one specific project only, or a continuing business relationship such as the Fuji Xerox _____.
   a. Joint Venture
   b. Patent
   c. Civil Rights Act of 1991
   d. Meritor Savings Bank v. Vinson

2. An _____ is a person who has possession of an enterprise and assumes significant accountability for the inherent risks and the outcome. It is an ambitious leader who combines land, labor, and capital to create and market new goods or services. The term is a loanword from French and was first defined by the Irish economist Richard Cantillon.
   a. A4e
   b. AAAI
   c. A Stake in the Outcome
   d. Entrepreneur

3. _____ is a form of social influence. It is the process of guiding people and oneself toward the adoption of an idea, attitude, or action by rational and symbolic (though not always logical) means. It is strategy of problem-solving relying on 'appeals' rather than coercion.
   a. Personal space
   b. Social loafing
   c. Self-enhancement
   d. Persuasion

4. An _____ is a person temporarily or permanently residing in a country and culture other than that of the person's upbringing or legal residence. The word comes from the Latin ex and patria (country, fatherland.)

The term is sometimes used in the context of Westerners living in non-Western countries, although it is also used to describe Westerners living in other Western countries, such as Americans living in the United Kingdom, or Britons living in Spain.

   a. A Stake in the Outcome
   b. AAAI
   c. A4e
   d. Expatriate

Chapter 5. Cross-cultural Negotiation and Decision Making

5. _____ is a forward looking process for setting goals and regularly checking progress toward achieving those goals. It is a continual feedback process whereby the actual outputs are measured and compared with the desired goals. Any discrepancy or gap is then fed back into changing the inputs of the process, so as to achieve the desired goals or outputs.
   a. Performance management
   b. 33 Strategies of War
   c. 1990 Clean Air Act
   d. 28-hour day

6. _____ is a set of values based on hard work and diligence. It is also a belief in the moral benefit of work and its ability to enhance character. An example would be the Protestant _____.
   a. 1990 Clean Air Act
   b. 33 Strategies of War
   c. Work ethic
   d. 28-hour day

7. _____ is a field of study that looks at how people from differing cultural backgrounds endeavour to communicate.

In years during and preceding the Cold War, the United States economy was largely self-contained because the world was polarized into two separate and competing powers: the east and west. However, changes and advancements in economic relationships, political systems, and technological options began to break down old cultural barriers.

   a. 33 Strategies of War
   b. 28-hour day
   c. 1990 Clean Air Act
   d. Cross-cultural communication

8. _____ is a range of processes aimed at alleviating or eliminating sources of conflict. The term '_____' is sometimes used interchangeably with the term dispute resolution or alternative dispute resolution. Processes of _____ generally include negotiation, mediation and diplomacy.
   a. 33 Strategies of War
   b. 28-hour day
   c. 1990 Clean Air Act
   d. Conflict resolution

Chapter 5. Cross-cultural Negotiation and Decision Making

9. _____ can be regarded as an outcome of mental processes (cognitive process) leading to the selection of a course of action among several alternatives. Every _____ process produces a final choice. The output can be an action or an opinion of choice.
   a. 33 Strategies of War
   b. 28-hour day
   c. Decision making
   d. 1990 Clean Air Act

10. A _____, in business matters, is an entity that is controlled by a bigger and more powerful entity. The controlled entity is called a company, corporation, or limited liability company and in some cases can be a government or state-owned enterprise, and the controlling entity is called its parent (or the parent company.) The reason for this distinction is that a lone company cannot be a _____ of any organization; only an entity representing a legal fiction as a separate entity can be a _____.
   a. 1990 Clean Air Act
   b. Subsidiary
   c. 28-hour day
   d. 33 Strategies of War

11. A _____ is one of several ways of doing research whether it is social science related or even socially related. It is an intensive study of a single group, incident, or community.Other ways include experiments, surveys, multiple histories, and analysis of archival information .

    Rather than using samples and following a rigid protocol to examine limited number of variables, _____ methods involve an in-depth, longitudinal examination of a single instance or event: a case.

   a. Case study
   b. 1990 Clean Air Act
   c. Standard operating procedure
   d. Longitudinal study

12. A _____ is a list of the general tasks and responsibilities of a position. Typically, it also includes to whom the position reports, specifications such as the qualifications needed by the person in the job, salary range for the position, etc. A _____ is usually developed by conducting a job analysis, which includes examining the tasks and sequences of tasks necessary to perform the job.
   a. Job description
   b. Recruitment advertising
   c. Recruitment
   d. Recruitment Process Insourcing

Chapter 6. Formulating Strategy

1. _____ is an organization's process of defining its strategy and making decisions on allocating its resources to pursue this strategy, including its capital and people. Various business analysis techniques can be used in _____, including SWOT analysis (Strengths, Weaknesses, Opportunities, and Threats) and PEST analysis (Political, Economic, Social, and Technological analysis) or STEER analysis involving Socio-cultural, Technological, Economic, Ecological, and Regulatory factors and EPISTEL (Environment, Political, Informatic, Social, Technological, Economic and Legal)

_____ is the formal consideration of an organization's future course. All _____ deals with at least one of three key questions:

1. 'What do we do?'
2. 'For whom do we do it?'
3. 'How do we excel?'

In business _____, the third question is better phrased 'How can we beat or avoid competition?'. (Bradford and Duncan, page 1.)

a. 28-hour day
b. 1990 Clean Air Act
c. 33 Strategies of War
d. Strategic planning

2. _____ as defined in business terms is an organization's strategic guide to globalization. A sound _____ should address these questions: what must be (versus what is) the extent of market presence in the world's major markets? How to build the necessary global presence? What must be (versus what is) the optimal locations around the world for the various value chain activities? How to run global presence into global competitive advantage?

Academic research on _____ came of age during the 1980s, including work by Michael Porter and Christopher Bartlett ' Sumantra Ghoshal. Among the forces perceived to bring about the globalization of competition were convergence in economic systems and technological change, especially in information technology, that facilitated and required the coordination of a multinational firm's strategy on a worldwide scale.

a. 1990 Clean Air Act
b. Global strategy
c. 28-hour day
d. 33 Strategies of War

3. _____ is a process of gathering, analyzing, and dispensing information for tactical or strategic purposes. The _____ process entails obtaining both factual and subjective information on the business environments in which a company is operating or considering entering.

Chapter 6. Formulating Strategy

There are three ways of scanning the business environment:

- Ad-hoc scanning - Short term, infrequent examinations usually initiated by a crisis
- Regular scanning - Studies done on a regular schedule (say, once a year)
- Continuous scanning(also called continuous learning) - continuous structured data collection and processing on a broad range of environmental factors

Most commentators feel that in today's turbulent business environment the best scanning method available is continuous scanning. This allows the firm to :

-act quickly-take advantage of opportunities before competitors do-respond to environmental threats before significant damage is done

   a. A4e
   b. A Stake in the Outcome
   c. AAAI
   d. Environmental scanning

4. _____ can be regarded as an outcome of mental processes (cognitive process) leading to the selection of a course of action among several alternatives. Every _____ process produces a final choice. The output can be an action or an opinion of choice.
   a. Decision making
   b. 28-hour day
   c. 1990 Clean Air Act
   d. 33 Strategies of War

5. In economics, _____ refers to the ability of a person or a country to produce a particular good at a lower marginal cost and opportunity cost than another person or country. It is the ability to produce a product most efficiently given all the other products that could be produced. It can be contrasted with absolute advantage which refers to the ability of a person or a country to produce a particular good at a lower absolute cost than another.
   a. 28-hour day
   b. 1990 Clean Air Act
   c. 33 Strategies of War
   d. Comparative advantage

Chapter 6. Formulating Strategy

6. _____ is a strategic planning method used to evaluate the Strengths, Weaknesses, Opportunities, and Threats involved in a project or in a business venture. It involves specifying the objective of the business venture or project and identifying the internal and external factors that are favorable and unfavorable to achieving that objective. The technique is credited to Albert Humphrey, who led a convention at Stanford University in the 1960s and 1970s using data from Fortune 500 companies.
   a. Corporate image
   b. Market share
   c. Marketing
   d. SWOT analysis

7. _____ in its literal sense is the process of transformation of local or regional phenomena into global ones. It can be described as a process by which the people of the world are unified into a single society and function together.

This process is a combination of economic, technological, sociocultural and political forces.

   a. Globalization
   b. Cost Management
   c. Histogram
   d. Collaborative Planning, Forecasting and Replenishment

8. The _____ is an economic tool used to determine the strategic resources available to a firm. The fundamental principle of the _____ is that the basis for a competitive advantage of a firm lies primarily in the application of the bundle of valuable resources at the firm's disposal (Wernerfelt, 1984, p172; Rumelt, 1984, p557-558.) To transform a short-run competitive advantage into a sustained competitive advantage requires that these resources are heterogeneous in nature and not perfectly mobile (Barney, 1991, p105-106; Peteraf, 1993, p180).
   a. Resource-based view
   b. Frenemy
   c. Business philosophy
   d. Catfish effect

9. _____ of the learning curve effect and the closely related experience curve effect express the relationship between equations for experience and efficiency or between efficiency gains and investment in the effort. The experience of 'learning curves' was first observed by the 19th Century German psychologist Hermann Ebbinghaus according to the difficulty of memorizing varying numbers of verbal stimuli, and subsequent learning about the complex processes of learning are discussed in the

The rule used for representing the learning curve effect states that the more times a task has been performed, the less time will be required on each subsequent iteration.

a. Models
b. Spatial Decision Support Systems
c. Point biserial correlation coefficient
d. Distribution

10. _____ describes commerce transactions between businesses, such as between a manufacturer and a wholesaler, or between a wholesaler and a retailer. Contrasting terms are business-to-consumer (B2C) and business-to-government (B2G.)

The volume of B2B transactions is much higher than the volume of B2C transactions.

a. Category management
b. Business-to-business
c. Product bundling
d. Market environment

11. _____, commonly referred to as 'eBusiness' or 'e-Business', may be defined as the utilization of information and communication technologies (ICT) in support of all the activities of business. Commerce constitutes the exchange of products and services between businesses, groups and individuals and hence can be seen as one of the essential activities of any business. Hence, electronic commerce or eCommerce focuses on the use of ICT to enable the external activities and relationships of the business with individuals, groups and other businesses .
a. AAAI
b. A Stake in the Outcome
c. A4e
d. Electronic business

12. _____ is exchange of capital, goods, and services across international borders or territories. In most countries, it represents a significant share of gross domestic product (GDP.) While _____ has been present throughout much of history , its economic, social, and political importance has been on the rise in recent centuries.
a. A Stake in the Outcome
b. A4e
c. AAAI
d. International trade

13. _____ refers to the methods of practicing and using another person's business philosophy. The franchisor grants the independent operator the right to distribute its products, techniques, and trademarks for a percentage of gross monthly sales and a royalty fee. Various tangibles and intangibles such as national or international advertising, training, and other support services are commonly made available by the franchisor.

Chapter 6. Formulating Strategy

   a. ServiceMaster
   b. 28-hour day
   c. 1990 Clean Air Act
   d. Franchising

14. _____ refers to the stock of skills and knowledge embodied in the ability to perform labor so as to produce economic value. It is the skills and knowledge gained by a worker through education and experience. Many early economic theories refer to it simply as labor, one of three factors of production, and consider it to be a fungible resource -- homogeneous and easily interchangeable.
   a. Productivity management
   b. Deflation
   c. Market structure
   d. Human capital

15. _____ describes the relocation by a company of a business process from one country to another -- typically an operational process, such as manufacturing such as accounting. Even state governments employ _____.

The term is in use in several distinct but closely related ways.

   a. A4e
   b. AAAI
   c. A Stake in the Outcome
   d. Offshoring

16. _____ is subcontracting a process, such as product design or manufacturing, to a third-party company. The decision to outsource is often made in the interest of lowering cost or making better use of time and energy costs, redirecting or conserving energy directed at the competencies of a particular business, or to make more efficient use of land, labor, capital, (information) technology and resources. _____ became part of the business lexicon during the 1980s.
   a. Operant conditioning
   b. Unemployment insurance
   c. Opinion leadership
   d. Outsourcing

17. A _____ is an entity formed between two or more parties to undertake economic activity together. The parties agree to create a new entity by both contributing equity, and they then share in the revenues, expenses, and control of the enterprise. The venture can be for one specific project only, or a continuing business relationship such as the Fuji Xerox _____.

Chapter 6. Formulating Strategy

a. Civil Rights Act of 1991
b. Meritor Savings Bank v. Vinson
c. Patent
d. Joint venture

18. An _____ is a person who has possession of an enterprise and assumes significant accountability for the inherent risks and the outcome. It is an ambitious leader who combines land, labor, and capital to create and market new goods or services. The term is a loanword from French and was first defined by the Irish economist Richard Cantillon.

   a. A4e
   b. AAAI
   c. A Stake in the Outcome
   d. Entrepreneur

19. _____ consists of the mental process of thinking involved with the process of judging the merits of multiple options and selecting one of them for action. Some simple examples include deciding whether to get up in the morning or go back to sleep, or selecting a given route for a journey. More complex examples (often decisions that affect what a person thinks or their core beliefs) include choosing a lifestyle, religious affiliation, or political position.

   a. Groups decision making
   b. Championship mobilization
   c. Trade study
   d. Choice

20. A _____ is a process that can allow an organization to concentrate its limited resources on the greatest opportunities to increase sales and achieve a sustainable competitive advantage. A _____ should be centered around the key concept that customer satisfaction is the main goal.

A _____ is a written plan which combines product development, promotion, distribution, and pricing approach, identifies the firm's marketing goals, and explains how they will be achieved within a stated timeframe.

   a. Disruptive technology
   b. Marketing strategy
   c. Category management
   d. Product bundling

Chapter 7. Global Alliances and Strategy Implementation

1. The phrase mergers and _____s refers to the aspect of corporate strategy, corporate finance and management dealing with the buying, selling and combining of different companies that can aid, finance, or help a growing company in a given industry grow rapidly without having to create another business entity.

An _____, also known as a takeover or a buyout, is the buying of one company (the 'target') by another. An _____ may be friendly or hostile.

a. Acquisition
b. AAAI
c. A Stake in the Outcome
d. A4e

2. A _____ is an entity formed between two or more parties to undertake economic activity together. The parties agree to create a new entity by both contributing equity, and they then share in the revenues, expenses, and control of the enterprise. The venture can be for one specific project only, or a continuing business relationship such as the Fuji Xerox _____.
a. Patent
b. Meritor Savings Bank v. Vinson
c. Civil Rights Act of 1991
d. Joint venture

3. A _____ is a formal relationship between two or more parties to pursue a set of agreed upon goals or to meet a critical business need while remaining independent organizations.

Partners may provide the _____ with resources such as products, distribution channels, manufacturing capability, project funding, capital equipment, knowledge, expertise, or intellectual property. The alliance is a cooperation or collaboration which aims for a synergy where each partner hopes that the benefits from the alliance will be greater than those from individual efforts.

a. Farmshoring
b. Strategic alliance
c. Golden parachute
d. Process automation

4. An _____ is a person who has possession of an enterprise and assumes significant accountability for the inherent risks and the outcome. It is an ambitious leader who combines land, labor, and capital to create and market new goods or services. The term is a loanword from French and was first defined by the Irish economist Richard Cantillon.

Chapter 7. Global Alliances and Strategy Implementation

a. A4e
b. AAAI
c. Entrepreneur
d. A Stake in the Outcome

5. _____ is a term used to describe practice of sourcing from the global market for goods and services across geopolitical boundaries. _____ often aims to exploit global efficiencies in the delivery of a product or service. These efficiencies include low cost skilled labor, low cost raw material and other economic factors like tax breaks and low trade tariffs.
   a. 1990 Clean Air Act
   b. Purchasing process
   c. Purchase requisition
   d. Global sourcing

6. In business, the term word _____ refers to a number of procurement practices, aimed at finding, evaluating and engaging suppliers of goods and services:

   - Global _____, a procurement strategy aimed at exploiting global efficiencies in production
   - Strategic _____, a component of supply chain management, for improving and re-evaluating purchasing activities
   - _____, the identification of job candidates through proactive recruiting technique
   - Co-_____, a type of auditing service
   - Low-cost country _____, a procurement strategy for acquiring materials from countries with lower labour and production costs in order to cut operating expenses
   - Corporate _____, a supply chain, purchasing/procurement, and inventory function
   - Second-tier _____, a practice of rewarding suppliers for attempting to achieve minority-owned business spending goals of their customer
   - Netsourcing, a practice of utilizing an established group of businesses, individuals, or hardware ' software applications to streamline or initiate procurement practices by tapping in to and working through a third party provider
   - Inverted _____, a price volatility reduction strategy usually conducted by procurement or supply-chain person by which the value of an organization's waste-stream is maximized by actively seeking out the highest price possible from a range of potential buyers exploiting price trends and other market factors
   - Multisourcing, a strategy that treats a given function, such as IT, as a portfolio of activities, some of which should be outsourced and others of which should be performed by internal staff.
   - Crowdsourcing, using an undefined, generally large group of people or community in the form of an open call to perform a task

In journalism, it can also refer to:

   - Journalism _____, the practice of identifying a person or publication that gives information
   - Single _____, the reuse of content in publishing

Chapter 7. Global Alliances and Strategy Implementation

In computing, it can refer to:

- Open-_____, the act of releasing previously proprietary software under an open source/free software license
- Power _____ equipment, network devices that will provide power in a Power over Ethernet (PoE) setup

a. Continuous
b. Cost Management
c. Reinforcement
d. Sourcing

7. _____ is subcontracting a process, such as product design or manufacturing, to a third-party company. The decision to outsource is often made in the interest of lowering cost or making better use of time and energy costs, redirecting or conserving energy directed at the competencies of a particular business, or to make more efficient use of land, labor, capital, (information) technology and resources. _____ became part of the business lexicon during the 1980s.
   a. Outsourcing
   b. Unemployment insurance
   c. Opinion leadership
   d. Operant conditioning

8. _____ is one of the managerial functions like planning, organizing, staffing and directing. It is an important function because it helps to check the errors and to take the corrective action so that deviation from standards are minimized and stated goals of the organization are achieved in desired manner. According to modern concepts, _____ is a foreseeing action whereas earlier concept of _____ was used only when errors were detected. _____ in management means setting standards, measuring actual performance and taking corrective action.
   a. Schedule of reinforcement
   b. Control
   c. Decision tree pruning
   d. Turnover

9. _____ is a forward looking process for setting goals and regularly checking progress toward achieving those goals. It is a continual feedback process whereby the actual outputs are measured and compared with the desired goals. Any discrepancy or gap is then fed back into changing the inputs of the process, so as to achieve the desired goals or outputs.

Chapter 7. Global Alliances and Strategy Implementation

a. 33 Strategies of War
b. 28-hour day
c. 1990 Clean Air Act
d. Performance management

10. _____ comprises a range of practices used in an organisation to identify, create, represent, distribute and enable adoption of insights and experiences. Such insights and experiences comprise knowledge, either embodied in individuals or embedded in organisational processes or practice.

An established discipline since 1991, _____ includes courses taught in the fields of business administration, information systems, management, and library and information sciences.

a. 1990 Clean Air Act
b. 28-hour day
c. 33 Strategies of War
d. Knowledge management

11. _____, commonly known as e-commerce, consists of the buying and selling of products or services over electronic systems such as the Internet and other computer networks. The amount of trade conducted electronically has grown extraordinarily with widespread Internet usage. The use of commerce is conducted in this way, spurring and drawing on innovations in electronic funds transfer, supply chain management, Internet marketing, online transaction processing, electronic data interchange (EDI), inventory management systems, and automated data collection systems.

a. Online shopping
b. A4e
c. A Stake in the Outcome
d. Electronic Commerce

Chapter 8. Organization Structure and Control Systems

1. An _____ is a mostly hierarchical concept of subordination of entities that collaborate and contribute to serve one common aim.

Organizations are a variant of clustered entities. The structure of an organization is usually set up in many a styles, dependent on their objectives and ambience.

- a. Open shop
- b. Organizational structure
- c. Organizational development
- d. Informal organization

2. A _____ or transnational corporation is a corporation or enterprise that manages production or delivers services in more than one country. It can also be referred to as an international corporation.

The first modern _____ is generally thought to be the Dutch East India Company, established in 1602.

- a. Financial Accounting Standards Board
- b. Small and medium enterprises
- c. Command center
- d. Multinational corporation

3. _____ is understood as a business unit within the overall corporate identity which is distinguishable from other business because it serves a defined external market where management can conduct strategic planning in relation to products and markets. When companies become really large, they are best thought of as being composed of a number of businesses (or _____s.)

In the broader domain of strategic management, the phrase '_____' came into use in the 1960s, largely as a result of General Electric's many units.

- a. Strategic business unit
- b. Switching cost
- c. Strategic drift
- d. Strategic group

4. _____ in its literal sense is the process of transformation of local or regional phenomena into global ones. It can be described as a process by which the people of the world are unified into a single society and function together.

This process is a combination of economic, technological, sociocultural and political forces.

Chapter 8. Organization Structure and Control Systems

a. Histogram
b. Cost Management
c. Globalization
d. Collaborative Planning, Forecasting and Replenishment

5. A _____ is an entity formed between two or more parties to undertake economic activity together. The parties agree to create a new entity by both contributing equity, and they then share in the revenues, expenses, and control of the enterprise. The venture can be for one specific project only, or a continuing business relationship such as the Fuji Xerox _____.
   a. Civil Rights Act of 1991
   b. Meritor Savings Bank v. Vinson
   c. Patent
   d. Joint Venture

6. An _____ is a person who has possession of an enterprise and assumes significant accountability for the inherent risks and the outcome. It is an ambitious leader who combines land, labor, and capital to create and market new goods or services. The term is a loanword from French and was first defined by the Irish economist Richard Cantillon.
   a. A4e
   b. AAAI
   c. A Stake in the Outcome
   d. Entrepreneur

7. Procter is a surname, and may also refer to:

   - Bryan Waller Procter (pseud. Barry Cornwall), English poet
   - Goodwin Procter, American law firm
   - _____, consumer products multinational

a. Strict liability
b. Master and Servant Acts
c. Downstream
d. Procter ' Gamble

8. _____ consists of the mental process of thinking involved with the process of judging the merits of multiple options and selecting one of them for action. Some simple examples include deciding whether to get up in the morning or go back to sleep, or selecting a given route for a journey. More complex examples (often decisions that affect what a person thinks or their core beliefs) include choosing a lifestyle, religious affiliation, or political position.

a. Championship mobilization
b. Trade study
c. Groups decision making
d. Choice

9. _____ can be regarded as an outcome of mental processes (cognitive process) leading to the selection of a course of action among several alternatives. Every _____ process produces a final choice. The output can be an action or an opinion of choice.
a. Decision making
b. 28-hour day
c. 1990 Clean Air Act
d. 33 Strategies of War

10. _____ is one of the managerial functions like planning, organizing, staffing and directing. It is an important function because it helps to check the errors and to take the corrective action so that deviation from standards are minimized and stated goals of the organization are achieved in desired manner. According to modern concepts, _____ is a foreseeing action whereas earlier concept of _____ was used only when errors were detected. _____ in management means setting standards, measuring actual performance and taking corrective action.
a. Decision tree pruning
b. Schedule of reinforcement
c. Control
d. Turnover

11. A _____ is a formal relationship between two or more parties to pursue a set of agreed upon goals or to meet a critical business need while remaining independent organizations.

Partners may provide the _____ with resources such as products, distribution channels, manufacturing capability, project funding, capital equipment, knowledge, expertise, or intellectual property. The alliance is a cooperation or collaboration which aims for a synergy where each partner hopes that the benefits from the alliance will be greater than those from individual efforts.

a. Golden parachute
b. Farmshoring
c. Process automation
d. Strategic alliance

Chapter 9. Staffing, Training, and Compensation for Global Operations

1. An _____ is a person temporarily or permanently residing in a country and culture other than that of the person's upbringing or legal residence. The word comes from the Latin ex and patria (country, fatherland.)

The term is sometimes used in the context of Westerners living in non-Western countries, although it is also used to describe Westerners living in other Western countries, such as Americans living in the United Kingdom, or Britons living in Spain.

   a. A4e
   b. A Stake in the Outcome
   c. Expatriate
   d. AAAI

2. _____ is a field of study that looks at how people from differing cultural backgrounds endeavour to communicate.

In years during and preceding the Cold War, the United States economy was largely self-contained because the world was polarized into two separate and competing powers: the east and west. However, changes and advancements in economic relationships, political systems, and technological options began to break down old cultural barriers.

   a. 33 Strategies of War
   b. Cross-cultural communication
   c. 1990 Clean Air Act
   d. 28-hour day

3. _____ is a forward looking process for setting goals and regularly checking progress toward achieving those goals. It is a continual feedback process whereby the actual outputs are measured and compared with the desired goals. Any discrepancy or gap is then fed back into changing the inputs of the process, so as to achieve the desired goals or outputs.
   a. 33 Strategies of War
   b. 28-hour day
   c. 1990 Clean Air Act
   d. Performance management

4. A _____ or transnational corporation is a corporation or enterprise that manages production or delivers services in more than one country. It can also be referred to as an international corporation.

The first modern _____ is generally thought to be the Dutch East India Company, established in 1602.

a. Multinational corporation
b. Command center
c. Financial Accounting Standards Board
d. Small and medium enterprises

5. A _____ is an entity formed between two or more parties to undertake economic activity together. The parties agree to create a new entity by both contributing equity, and they then share in the revenues, expenses, and control of the enterprise. The venture can be for one specific project only, or a continuing business relationship such as the Fuji Xerox _____.

   a. Meritor Savings Bank v. Vinson
   b. Civil Rights Act of 1991
   c. Patent
   d. Joint Venture

6. An _____ is a person who has possession of an enterprise and assumes significant accountability for the inherent risks and the outcome. It is an ambitious leader who combines land, labor, and capital to create and market new goods or services. The term is a loanword from French and was first defined by the Irish economist Richard Cantillon.

   a. AAAI
   b. A Stake in the Outcome
   c. A4e
   d. Entrepreneur

7. _____ is the strategic and coherent approach to the management of an organisation's most valued assets - the people working there who individually and collectively contribute to the achievement of the objectives of the business. The terms '_____' and 'human resources' (HR) have largely replaced the term 'personnel management' as a description of the processes involved in managing people in organizations. In simple sense, _____ means employing people, developing their resources, utilizing, maintaining and compensating their services in tune with the job and organizational requirement.

   a. Revolving door syndrome
   b. Progressive discipline
   c. Job knowledge
   d. Human Resource Management

Chapter 9. Staffing, Training, and Compensation for Global Operations 33

8. _____ refers to the movement of cash into or out of a business or financial product. It is usually measured during a specified, finite period of time. Measurement of _____ can be used

- to determine a project's rate of return or value. The time of _____s into and out of projects are used as inputs in financial models such as internal rate of return, and net present value.
- to determine problems with a business's liquidity. Being profitable does not necessarily mean being liquid. A company can fail because of a shortage of cash, even while profitable.
- as an alternate measure of a business's profits when it is believed that accrual accounting concepts do not represent economic realities. For example, a company may be notionally profitable but generating little operational cash (as may be the case for a company that barters its products rather than selling for cash.) In such a case, the company may be deriving additional operating cash by issuing shares evaluating default risk, re-investment requirements, etc.

_____ is a generic term used differently depending on the context. It may be defined by users for their own purposes.

a. Gross profit margin
b. Sweat equity
c. Gross profit
d. Cash flow

9. In sociology, anthropology and cultural studies, a _____ is a group of people with a culture (whether distinct or hidden) which differentiates them from the larger culture to which they belong. If a particular _____ is characterized by a systematic opposition to the dominant culture, it may be described as a counterculture.

As early as 1950, David Riesman distinguished between a majority, 'which passively accepted commercially provided styles and meanings, and a '_____' which actively sought a minority style ...

a. 33 Strategies of War
b. 28-hour day
c. 1990 Clean Air Act
d. Subculture

10. In financial accounting, a _____ or statement of financial position is a summary of a person's or organization's balances. Assets, liabilities and ownership equity are listed as of a specific date, such as the end of its financial year. A _____ is often described as a snapshot of a company's financial condition.

a. 33 Strategies of War
b. 1990 Clean Air Act
c. Balance sheet
d. 28-hour day

11. The term '_____' refers to the concept of collecting information and attempting to spot a pattern in the information. In some fields of study, the term '_____' has more formally-defined meanings.

In project management _____ is a mathematical technique that uses historical results to predict future outcome.

   a. Least squares
   b. Stepwise regression
   c. Regression analysis
   d. Trend analysis

Chapter 10. Developing a Global Management Cadre

1. An _____ is a person temporarily or permanently residing in a country and culture other than that of the person's upbringing or legal residence. The word comes from the Latin ex and patria (country, fatherland.)

The term is sometimes used in the context of Westerners living in non-Western countries, although it is also used to describe Westerners living in other Western countries, such as Americans living in the United Kingdom, or Britons living in Spain.

   a. A Stake in the Outcome
   b. AAAI
   c. Expatriate
   d. A4e

2. The _____ is the labour pool in employment. It is generally used to describe those working for a single company or industry, but can also apply to a geographic region like a city, country, state, etc. The term generally excludes the employers or management, and implies those involved in manual labour.
   a. Workforce
   b. Division of labour
   c. Work-life balance
   d. Pink-collar worker

3. _____ is a term defined by the Oxford English Dictionary as an individual's 'course or progress through life '. It is usually considered to pertain to remunerative work (and sometimes also formal education.)

The etymology of the term is somewhat ironic in that it comes from the Latin word carrera, which means race .

   a. Spatial mismatch
   b. Career planning
   c. Career
   d. Nursing shortage

Chapter 10. Developing a Global Management Cadre

4. _____ is defined by Ball (1997) as:

   1. Making career choices and decisions - the traditional focus of careers interventions. The changed nature of work means that individuals may now have to revisit this process more frequently now and in the future, more than in the past.
   2. Managing the organizational career - concerns the _____ tasks of individuals within the workplace, such as decision-making, life-stage transitions, dealing with stress etc.
   3. Managing 'boundaryless' careers - refers to skills needed by workers whose employment is beyond the boundaries of a single organisation, a workstyle common among, for example, artists and designers.
   4. Taking control of one's personal development - as employers take less responsibility, employees need to take control of their own development in order to maintain and enhance their employability.

Career planning is a subset of _____. Career planning applies the concepts of Strategic planning and Marketing to taking charge of one's professional future.

   a. Job interview
   b. Job fair
   c. Psychological contract
   d. Career management

5. A _____ is directly responsible for managing the day-to-day operations (and profitability) of a company.

   Chief Executive Officer (CEO)
   - As the top manager, the CEO is typically responsible for the entire operations of the corporation and reports directly to the chairman and board of directors. It is the CEO's responsibility to implement board decisions and initiatives and to maintain the smooth operation of the firm, with the assistance of senior management.

   a. Field service management
   b. Vorstand
   c. Management team
   d. Getting Things Done

6. _____ is a forward looking process for setting goals and regularly checking progress toward achieving those goals. It is a continual feedback process whereby the actual outputs are measured and compared with the desired goals. Any discrepancy or gap is then fed back into changing the inputs of the process, so as to achieve the desired goals or outputs.

a. 28-hour day
b. 33 Strategies of War
c. 1990 Clean Air Act
d. Performance management

7. A _____ is one scenario provided for evaluation by respondents in a Choice Experiment. Responses are collected and used to create a Choice Model. Respondents are usually provided with a series of differing _____s for evaluation.
   a. Computerized classification test
   b. Pairwise comparison
   c. Choice Set
   d. Thurstone scale

8. The field of _____ looks at the relationship between management and workers, particularly groups of workers represented by a union.

_____ is an important factor in analyzing 'varieties of capitalism', such as neocorporatism, social democracy, and neoliberalism

   a. Overtime
   b. Organizational effectiveness
   c. Informal organization
   d. Industrial relations

9. The _____ is a trilateral trade bloc in North America created by the governments of the United States, Canada, and Mexico. The agreement creating the trade bloc came into force on January 1, 1994. It superseded the Canada-United States Free Trade Agreement between the U.S. and Canada.
   a. Business war game
   b. Trade union
   c. Career portfolios
   d. North American Free Trade Agreement

10. In organized labor, _____ is the method whereby workers organize together (usually in unions) to meet, converse, and negotiate upon the work conditions with their employers normally resulting in a written contract setting forth the wages, hours, and other conditions to be observed for a stipulated period.It is the practice in which union and company representatives meet to negotiate a new labor contract. In various national labor and employment law contexts, the term _____ takes on a more specific legal meaning. In a broad sense, however, it is the coming together of workers to negotiate their employment.

Chapter 10. Developing a Global Management Cadre

a. Labor rights
b. Labour law
c. Collective bargaining
d. Paid time off

11. _____ is a type of trade policy that allows traders to act and transact without interference from government. Thus, the policy permits trading partners mutual gains from trade, with goods and services produced according to the theory of comparative advantage.

Under a _____ policy, prices are a reflection of true supply and demand, and are the sole determinant of resource allocation.

a. Free Trade
b. 33 Strategies of War
c. 1990 Clean Air Act
d. 28-hour day

12. _____ is a designated group of countries that have agreed to eliminate tariffs, quotas and preferences on most (if not all) goods and services traded between them. It can be considered the second stage of economic integration. Countries choose this kind of economic integration form if their economical structures are complementary.

a. 33 Strategies of War
b. 1990 Clean Air Act
c. Free trade area
d. 28-hour day

13. _____ is a practice whereby the employees have a role in management of a company. The word is a somewhat clumsy and literal translation from the German word Mitbestimmung. _____ rights are different in different legal environments.

a. Decentralization
b. Management team
c. Business Process Improvement
d. Co-determination

Chapter 11. Motivating and Leading

1. Within graph theory and network analysis, there are various measures of the _____ of a vertex within a graph that determine the relative importance of a vertex within the graph (for example, how important a person is within a social network, or, in the theory of space syntax, how important a room is within a building or how well-used a road is within an urban network.)

There are four measures of _____ that are widely used in network analysis: degree _____, betweenness, closeness, and eigenvector _____.

The first, and simplest, is degree _____.

   a. 28-hour day
   b. 1990 Clean Air Act
   c. 33 Strategies of War
   d. Centrality

2. A _____ or transnational corporation is a corporation or enterprise that manages production or delivers services in more than one country. It can also be referred to as an international corporation.

The first modern _____ is generally thought to be the Dutch East India Company, established in 1602.

   a. Financial Accounting Standards Board
   b. Small and medium enterprises
   c. Command center
   d. Multinational corporation

3. _____ is a set of values based on hard work and diligence. It is also a belief in the moral benefit of work and its ability to enhance character. An example would be the Protestant _____.
   a. 28-hour day
   b. 1990 Clean Air Act
   c. 33 Strategies of War
   d. Work ethic

4. In neuroscience, the _____ is a collection of brain structures which attempts to regulate and control behavior by inducing pleasurable effects.

A psychological reward is a process that reinforces behavior -- something that, when offered, causes a behavior to increase in intensity. Reward is an operational concept for describing the positive value an individual ascribes to an object, behavioral act or an internal physical state.

Chapter 11. Motivating and Leading

   a. 28-hour day
   b. 33 Strategies of War
   c. Reward system
   d. 1990 Clean Air Act

5. A _____ is an entity formed between two or more parties to undertake economic activity together. The parties agree to create a new entity by both contributing equity, and they then share in the revenues, expenses, and control of the enterprise. The venture can be for one specific project only, or a continuing business relationship such as the Fuji Xerox _____.
   a. Civil Rights Act of 1991
   b. Patent
   c. Meritor Savings Bank v. Vinson
   d. Joint venture

6. An _____ is a person who has possession of an enterprise and assumes significant accountability for the inherent risks and the outcome. It is an ambitious leader who combines land, labor, and capital to create and market new goods or services. The term is a loanword from French and was first defined by the Irish economist Richard Cantillon.
   a. Entrepreneur
   b. A Stake in the Outcome
   c. AAAI
   d. A4e

7. An _____ is a person temporarily or permanently residing in a country and culture other than that of the person's upbringing or legal residence. The word comes from the Latin ex and patria (country, fatherland.)

The term is sometimes used in the context of Westerners living in non-Western countries, although it is also used to describe Westerners living in other Western countries, such as Americans living in the United Kingdom, or Britons living in Spain.

   a. A4e
   b. A Stake in the Outcome
   c. AAAI
   d. Expatriate

8. _____ is a forward looking process for setting goals and regularly checking progress toward achieving those goals. It is a continual feedback process whereby the actual outputs are measured and compared with the desired goals. Any discrepancy or gap is then fed back into changing the inputs of the process, so as to achieve the desired goals or outputs.

Chapter 11. Motivating and Leading

a. 28-hour day
b. Performance management
c. 33 Strategies of War
d. 1990 Clean Air Act

9. _____ has been described as the 'process of social influence in which one person can enlist the aid and support of others in the accomplishment of a common task' . A definition more inclusive of followers comes from Alan Keith of Genentech who said '_____ is ultimately about creating a way for people to contribute to making something extraordinary happen.'

_____ is one of the most salient aspects of the organizational context. However, defining _____ has been challenging.

a. 1990 Clean Air Act
b. 28-hour day
c. Situational leadership
d. Leadership

10. _____ can be regarded as an outcome of mental processes (cognitive process) leading to the selection of a course of action among several alternatives. Every _____ process produces a final choice. The output can be an action or an opinion of choice.
a. 28-hour day
b. 1990 Clean Air Act
c. 33 Strategies of War
d. Decision making

11. _____ refers to the movement of cash into or out of a business or financial product. It is usually measured during a specified, finite period of time. Measurement of _____ can be used

- to determine a project's rate of return or value. The time of _____s into and out of projects are used as inputs in financial models such as internal rate of return, and net present value.
- to determine problems with a business's liquidity. Being profitable does not necessarily mean being liquid. A company can fail because of a shortage of cash, even while profitable.
- as an alternate measure of a business's profits when it is believed that accrual accounting concepts do not represent economic realities. For example, a company may be notionally profitable but generating little operational cash (as may be the case for a company that barters its products rather than selling for cash.) In such a case, the company may be deriving additional operating cash by issuing shares evaluating default risk, re-investment requirements, etc.

_____ is a generic term used differently depending on the context. It may be defined by users for their own purposes.

a. Sweat equity
b. Gross profit
c. Gross profit margin
d. Cash flow

12. _____ is an advertisement in which a particular product specifically mentions a competitor by name for the express purpose of showing why the competitor is inferior to the product naming it.

This should not be confused with parody advertisements, where a fictional product is being advertised for the purpose of poking fun at the particular advertisement, nor should it be confused with the use of a coined brand name for the purpose of comparing the product without actually naming an actual competitor. ('Wikipedia tastes better and is less filling than the Encyclopedia Galactica.')

In the 1980s, during what has been referred to as the cola wars, soft-drink manufacturer Pepsi ran a series of advertisements where people, caught on hidden camera, in a blind taste test, chose Pepsi over rival Coca-Cola.

a. 1990 Clean Air Act
b. 28-hour day
c. 33 Strategies of War
d. Comparative advertising

13. _____ in its literal sense is the process of transformation of local or regional phenomena into global ones. It can be described as a process by which the people of the world are unified into a single society and function together.

This process is a combination of economic, technological, sociocultural and political forces.

a. Globalization
b. Histogram
c. Collaborative Planning, Forecasting and Replenishment
d. Cost Management

ANSWER KEY

Chapter 1
1. c   2. d   3. d   4. d   5. d   6. d   7. c   8. b   9. d   10. a
11. c   12. a   13. a   14. d   15. d   16. d

Chapter 2
1. d   2. d   3. d   4. c   5. d   6. b   7. a   8. d   9. b   10. d
11. d   12. d   13. a   14. b

Chapter 3
1. d   2. d   3. d   4. a   5. c   6. b   7. d   8. d   9. c

Chapter 4
1. b   2. c   3. c   4. a

Chapter 5
1. a   2. d   3. d   4. d   5. a   6. c   7. d   8. d   9. c   10. b
11. a   12. a

Chapter 6
1. d   2. b   3. d   4. a   5. d   6. d   7. a   8. a   9. a   10. b
11. d   12. d   13. d   14. d   15. d   16. d   17. d   18. d   19. d   20. b

Chapter 7
1. a   2. d   3. b   4. c   5. d   6. d   7. a   8. b   9. d   10. d
11. d

Chapter 8
1. b   2. d   3. a   4. c   5. d   6. d   7. d   8. d   9. a   10. c
11. d

Chapter 9
1. c   2. b   3. d   4. a   5. d   6. d   7. d   8. d   9. d   10. c
11. d

Chapter 10
1. c   2. a   3. c   4. d   5. c   6. d   7. c   8. d   9. d   10. c
11. a   12. c   13. d

Chapter 11
1. d   2. d   3. d   4. c   5. d   6. a   7. d   8. b   9. d   10. d
11. d   12. d   13. a

www.ingramcontent.com/pod-product-compliance
Lightning Source LLC
Chambersburg PA
CBHW080744250426
43671CB00038B/2866